i am tired of being a dandelion

zane frederick

central
avenue
publishing

2021

Published by Central Avenue Publishing, an imprint of Central Avenue Marketing Ltd.
www.centralavenuepublishing.com

i am tired of being a dandelion

Trade Paperback: 978-1-77168-243-5
Epub: 978-1-77168-244-2
Mobi: 978-1-77168-245-9

Published in Canada
Printed in United States of America

1. POETRY / General   2. POETRY / LGBT

10 9 8 7 6 5 4 3 2 1

to the ones who still wish on expired stars

to the dandelions that have been blown away

to the dreams that will only ever be dreams

i am
tired
of
being
a
dandelion

where hope lives

there is a place i
dream of often,
a place where i take
up more space,
don't walk as off,
purse my lips as if
no worries fill my head,
look people in the eye and
crack a smile out of cement,
a place where light comes from
somewhere other than the sky.

overanalyzing

why do i always seem
to read welcome signs
on doors that
remain locked?

the first step

i suppose i do not write to forget you
but rather to remind myself
why i need to.

i grab two, just in case

there are not enough
fortune cookies or shooting stars
to reassure me that love
will play out nice for me.

iridescent

we rode that bus in silence.
lights flashed after a stop
that wasn't ours and we
glanced at each other three times
before it went dark.

you ran off at your stop
in the middle of the
pouring rain.
i always caught your eye
but didn't catch a name.

through the tunnel

holding my breath

when you walk by,

i'll take my breath away

before you can.

reserved

how could i risk getting too close

to those lips when we both know

they belong to someone else?

vacancy

fate is a two-way street and i keep drifting

into the other lane, blowing through

the stop signs and every red light.

i must be turning down all the wrong roads.

i must be walking out of the same door, empty-handed.

the christmas with no gifts.

the birthday with no candles.

the new year's with no kiss.

favorites

i can't wait to tell
someone all of my
favorite things,
movies and books
and places to sit,
paintings and fruits
and cities to visit,
tell them about
my life before twenty
and all my biggest
dreams, all the art
i wish to see, and
hope they never leave.

uncertainty

flush my cheeks and shoot a risk
with a smile from across the room.
leave a napkin with a number
stained with hope and a chance.
the waiting is so long for a call
that will never come. head down
with my back against the wall.
i would rather have you say no
than to never know at all.

wasting the waiting

if it is meant to be
it will happen,

but i wish it did not
have to take this long
for me to wait and see
if it would become something
that it was never going to be.

rapunzel cuts her hair

i never understand why
i plan so far ahead for something
that is not in clear view.
creating fantasies and expectations
of a prince who has not saved me yet,
his horse going in the wrong direction
while i'm trapped in the tower of my mind,
waiting for someone to stop by.

empty-handed

i'm standing in the middle of a crowded

place and my hands sway in vacancy.

strangers fumble through vinyls and CDs,

stare at my lonely, and i can't wait to leave.

see how my friends have found hands to hold

while mine swing patiently

and i imagine, just once, a love that would

reach out for them, or even wait for me.

mystical mournings

cupid's bow does not

shoot stars anymore,

only eyes i cannot catch

and names that will

never taste my lips.

could i have just one more memory?

it is a choice to think about you still,

to have the past packed up in

the attic of my mind, a reminder

that some things will never leave.

and i believe storing you in thoughts

may continue to be an excuse to call this love

before a new season breezes through my window.

i won't stop looking through old frames

until i find new pictures to put in them.

muscle memory

i told you there were too many versions of far away
that needed to be put in place so i could move on without
somehow taking you with me.

when people asked about us, or how i was doing,
i swallowed swords. i said i was doing fine when i was
far from it. i said we talked less. spoke of you in the
past tense, as if there were a funeral they had missed.
you are more alive than ever, but i have been trying to kill
the idea of you. a big, beautiful machete and infatuation
to set on fire, but i forget to mention how you continue
to sit crisscross applesauce inside my pocket. i grab you
like car keys.

like muscle memory.

like i can't leave without you.

if i were to meet you downtown

i hold on when i shouldn't.
i'll lose circulation
before i ever lose you.

we speak in passing.
in wishing i asked how
your senior year went
and in crosswalks that took us away.

you drift down the alley of people
and i catch up with my friends while
looking back at the crowd.

kauai

was hawaii nice? i should have asked him,
because i know that he has never been.
i should have asked about the weather and
if the water is warm enough to swim.

i miss him when i know i'm not supposed to
so i shout it somewhere over the edge.
my tongue is tied in a Boy Scout knot
to help me swallow what i've never said.

i should have apologized for expecting too much
and for assuming he was drawn to men.
i should have been the first to place some distance
so it wouldn't hurt all of a sudden.

long distance

when i moved cities

    to get away from you

        i traveled lightly,

            brought my fondest

                moments in a carry-on.

                    just enough

                      to get by.

you have been
too many
last poems

sleeping hungry

i'm starting to look
like my old self again
but in a body that isn't mine.

i continue to sit in the belly of my lonely
as i watch past loves find other mouths to feed,
gnawing away at the crumbs they leave behind.

fulfillment

i ache for the pain
of your rejection.
i would rather hurt
in all of your noes
than to be buried
in all my alone.

that laugh sounded like safety

it was like hearing sirens,
a laugh as loud as an
ambulance when it
flashed in the rearview
mirror of my mind.
i moved out of the way
and i hated the way that felt,
watching the laughter
speed away from me
while it went to save
someone else.

and many more

as each year passes,
i wonder if you will wish me
a happy birthday again.
i wonder how old i will
turn when you stop.
i could receive all
the wishes in the world,
every genie could fill
their lamp up to the brim,
every twisted candle
could burn in my honor
and none of them would
feel as sincere as yours.
i look for your wish in
those bright specks in the sky
when they turn me
twenty at 9:28 p.m.
i wonder if you remember
my birthday anymore.
i wonder if you even
wish me happy.

hibiscus tea in the back room

i visit a place that reeks
of cigarettes and coffee grounds
and your name gets tossed around,
floats amongst heavy conversations
where i pick up the air pockets i hear it in,
and i know it's not you, just a different someone.

then i leave that place with an aftertaste of you
on the tip of my tongue.

someone has to be honest

just because i want
you to come back
doesn't mean you will,
and i probably shouldn't
say this but i can't help
that i think of you, still.

i'm always exhaling

i have climbed desert mountains

but your lungs still have my breath.

what more is there to get over?

what else is left?

l.a.

i'm up

on a rooftop

bar and i'm just ten

months shy of twenty-one.

the rum tastes like your bottom lip

and now you've got me coming undone.

boy, i loved you even then and i love

you even now, all your reckless

and your freckles and

the way you get

me down.

letting go is overrated

it's singing to their favorite album
until your throat is a rusted trumpet /
it's nights where you take the long way home /
drive past their house to see if the lights are still on /
it's finding an excuse to drag out the hurt
like waiting for them to hang up first /
it's dropping boulders down mountains
or skipping rocks in a lake / sometimes it's
diving in to pick them back up /
it's sprinkling salt in the wound
to make it burn one last time

tell me how to
love someone new
without letting
go of (you)

our finale

the last day i saw you was an average one.
summer wind with a handful of stars
on a lit-up backyard where i did not think
you would be, and then you were
and my lungs took a break.

they have been holding their breath
for two years now while i keep up with
your life through pictures and stories i
don't want to hear but listen to anyway
because it is all i have left.

that last day is still a wine stain
on all the calendars i hang up.

is it ever really over?

how dare i long for you?
the earth is tired of spinning
me around the sun, and i've lost count
of how many steps we've taken
away from each other.

i let time distance our last conversation
in light years, and i still carry the embers
in my mouth when fire falls from the sky.

i burn my tongue calling for you.

when i imagine my first name
paired with your last

i pretend it has a ring to it.

i imagine how it will look on christmas cards

and wedding invitations,

how it will taste when i say

it out loud or when i write it

on checks and emails

and thank-you letters.

i'll use my favorite pen

and practice my signature,

how to dot the i or

curl the last letter,

how to make it look sweet.

i'll still pretend it sounds right.

something pretty

i knew from the start you never

liked the same anatomy.

i scraped the apology off my tongue

when i made you out to be the boy-

-who-stayed in all of my reveries,

the face in all my wet dreams, and

i'll spend forever apologizing for keeping

you nestled in my mind. i folded the

words i dropped on your floor nicely,

hung them back in your closet for days

you decide to wear something pretty.

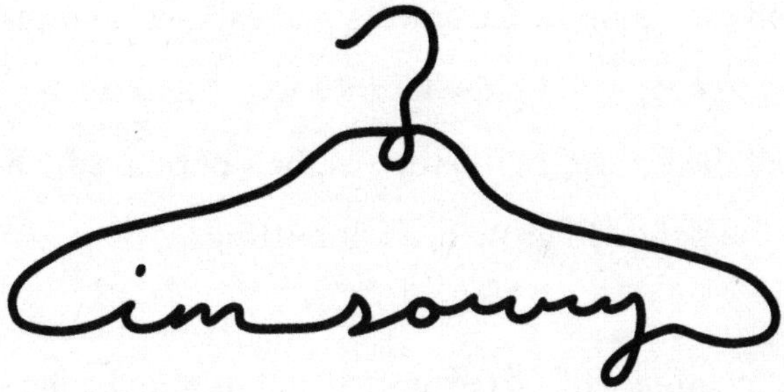
im sorry

and when you're gone

there will be a day when i have nothing left from you.
dusted out of all the basements and cabinets and places
i tried to keep you in. the injuries won't look as familiar
and all the bruises will return to their normal pale hue.
even the pain will grow tired of hurting.

and i'm sure i will drive by sites that used to be ours.
i'm sure they will be covered in new apartment
complexes or patches of grass that grow over our past
before i allow myself to.

i'm sure i will recall the memories, but i won't remember
how they felt. like playing piano for years only to be
pulled away and when you return, you still remember
the electricity on our fingers skipping across the keys.
now they just slow dance, flicking a string to the tune of
what used to be.

lonely compasses

i'm a north star and i keep looking
south for a speck of blue somewhere.
i can almost taste it.

someone once said
you were looking for me;

most days i hope you still are.

in every november

i have pulled muscles letting go,
and there's no use missing you in
small talk and when i remember
the daydreams and film scenes
we walked out of together.
i flash back to last days
when my friends said
i deserved better,
and i know if i
wait for you
i'll be here
forever.

surrender

it's supposed to happen
by chance or fate but
i throw my hands up.
too many what-ifs to
talk myself out of,
too many daydreams
have been discontinued,
expired expectations
and outdated wishes
that can no longer be renewed.

you never changed

winter took me with her crumpled leaves
the night i told you how i felt,
and when you said
you missed me i came back to tour spring,
but all the flowers looked the same.

what's the point of hummingbirds migrating
if there is nothing worth coming back for
once the snow stops?

after you

i can't stop you

from leaving but i

can ask you to hold

the door open for me

when you do

infinite

how many hopeless romantics
does it take to build a wall
high enough to keep
our hearts safe?

how many colors need to be
painted until it no longer looks
like your room in golden hour?

how many castles will it take us
to build before we start
believing in happy endings again?

generous

most times i wish we could

talk a little longer

until i pretend to forget why we quit.

because i want more,

and small talk is insufficient.

but with you i'll take what i can get.

i will survive

with any love

you provide

the harvest

all my meadows have caught fire and
the wind has stopped exhaling its exhaustion,
while i continue to blow dandelions
in your honor or pick off more petals
from flowers because i'll get to say
he loves me
more than once.

i don't want him to love me not.

self-discipline

i'll tie a string from my bedpost

to my hips when the hope starts

floating me up to a universe

where we work out,

and i can't promise i won't

cut the string and be left

suspended in midair,

because you make me

want to not come back down.

halfway

there have been loves
who only approach the
middle of my longing
before they retreat.
no brave legs have dared
to march across my entirety
without tripping over traps
that spark my anxiety,
so don't try and love me today
if you're only coming halfway.

what if he
loves me to
the moon
but never on
the way back?

blueprint for the broken

when they tell you they love you
they will only say it in every way
that isn't what you want it to mean,
and it will take everything in you
not to think otherwise.
being so sure of the wrong answer
is a blueprint for the broken.

if they want you then you won't
have to wonder how to make them.

if they love you then you won't have
to die a little each time you try to find proof.

snow in phoenix

arizona feels so lonesome

without you, dear.

in a heat wave

on this july day.

please come back here.

rooted

those barbed wires in the garden we grew looked like flowers, i swear. premature carnations and a dandelion tucked behind my ear. the seeds tickled the idea of something real stemming from all this. it felt like we never got enough sun. picked too early from the soil and dumped in borrowed water that would only last us so long. i always drank you up when nothing else sufficed.

i anticipated a hundred more rotations together, shoulder to shoulder. i pictured us back in your neighborhood park swinging out of rhythm with the gap between our hands,

almost always touching.

pittsburgh

and when i love

it's only ever

from far away

never close enough

to stay

on the lookout

wake me up before you leave so i don't have
to see the sunrise before i see you go.

this love is unpredictable and maybe that's the best part.

i sleep by the window and can't tell which direction you
are in, but the iron in my blood drags me south. i haven't
been on that side of you before but maybe i can catch
up. always grazing the skyline searching for blond hair
slicked back. i keep hitting my head on the atmosphere
and i never know which way i'm facing when you're not
around.

where does a balloon go after it floats away?

where do i put my hand after you let it go?

how it ends

some things are never resolved,
some questions never answered,
what-ifs dusted with the past.
sometimes closure
is a door left open.

why am i so good at ruining good things?

the flowers i bring home give up on me
before i can really breathe them in or place them
in a vase before they get bored.

i forget they still had some growing to do
before i pulled them out of the ground.
picked because i liked their color and their smell
and the way they look in the wind, though
i never took care of them enough
to make them stick around.

you're not supposed to find the one at nineteen

my father tells me this often,

though i am not in search of the one

but rather someone to show me

the paths in a forest i'm not sure

how to get lost in yet.

try to learn how to breathe in smoke

before i start the blaze.

try to learn how to survive a fire

before i light the match.

the hunter lets go

i want to know what it's
like to fall in love again
but i don't want it to
kill me on the way down.

i want to chase a butterfly
out of its garden and hope
it stays with me in the wild,
but i won't blame it for
going back to where
it came from, either.

the next one

what if i keep pulling on the fabric of fate

because i'm too afraid to see what becomes of nothing?

i see a train come along but this one doesn't feel right.

to let it pass as i sit for the next one, i don't mind the wait.

i let all these loves walk farther away

since it is safer for them to leave

than it is to stay.

slow, beating thing

who is going to love someone who turns into
a fire escape when i start smelling smoke?
who turns into an avalanche at a single touch
or a burnt-out lighthouse standing with
my hands rough and hair storm-tossed,
knowing a love is coming but i won't let it find me?
someone who can't let good things come into their life
because they leave as quickly as they come.

there are a million things i don't know how to be,

so tell me who is going to love this slow, beating thing?

it's exhausting being cautious

my arms are getting tired of holding up my guard

when you've had daisies in your holster this whole time.

i was born with a shotgun laughter and was never one

to aim well at the sky, but i will kiss you with the safety
off

when you spread your arms out wide,

pointing at your lips

saying hit me where it hurts.

come look

am i doing this right? come look / supervise / i'm trying
to give love / the centaur backs away / i'm holding
candied hearts as bait / come look / why is it so simple
for everyone else? / they sweep feet with grace and cupid
is running out of arrows / i don't think it's in it for me
/ not by fate or some made-up meant to be / that there
is someone to hold me firm / in all the right places / to
turn my stomach inside out / a feeling that breaks skin
/ i blister before you reach for my hand / come look / go
slow / then go for it

hurt in the hope

i break my fingers while crossing them
and pluck eyelashes off with care,
savoring every wish.

i can't keep losing parts of me
at the expense of a dream
that may not get to exist.

where my father doesn't walk me down the aisle

i stopped planning for my wedding
when i stopped believing that day would happen.

i carry a bouquet of burnt-out daydreams,
slow dance with fear and raise a toast
to all of my lonesome, fading evenings.
no more shooting stars or dragons.
no one on their way to save me.

eventually

the rose thorns convince me

that it's safer to be alone

than to be a burden

to someone's

good intentions.

every night i walk my lonely home

and before bed i pray that maybe

i won't always be a catastrophe,

that maybe i will fall asleep

to two heartbeats,

eventually.

i can only hope

it's there
for a split second,
a whiff of spring
and something real,
then it dies off,

rust and weight
falling to kiss
the pavement.

my knees hurt
from begging and
i'm tired of always
wanting to be saved.

anew

i'm an entire forest falling down
but no one turns to hear me.
i can be so much of myself
i think i am too heavy to carry.

i know i'm a lot at once
and something easy to outgrow,
to walk out of in silence.
i can hear them tiptoe.

i'll start over if i must
with echoes of a new soundtrack.
i swear that i'll fall right off the sidewalk
and promise to never come back.

hope
FULL

the bottom

they say there is a light
at the end of the tunnel.
that there is gold at the
bottom of every rainbow.
sometimes hope doesn't
come with luck or the sun;
it's just wishful thinking.
sometimes there is nothing
at the bottom to discover.

springfield

it's as if i am floating in the still of the unknown
and i don't know how to get to where i want to go.
i seem to miss out on the here and now
by wondering about tomorrow and not knowing how
to be the person i am trying to become.
i'll turn into an entire storm front,
but where do i start from?

i can't remember if you winked at me

my memories cry rose water on their worst days.

when they can't remember all the tender acts you did

or all the gentle words you said.

you are starting to dry up on my sidewalks

when you used to be a rainstorm

in all my afternoons.

as i pass by

his pupils were telescopes
always pointing down, and it's like
i'm floating when i pass by his street.
magic like me only happens
once every so often.

i have always been a comet
but he was never looking up.

hope

it's the only hand
i've ever been able
to comfortably hold,
the hand that never lets go.

more

if you don't like
the way i love you
then why do you
keep coming back?

serendipity

the pacific sighs when i call out your name,

sways her hair over my feet, drags me out

past my ankles, and i drop to my knees for the moon.

the tides try to stop me from following

the arch of color that hangs above me, but

i can't go home without knowing if

you were waiting there at the end,

covered in gold.

everywhere

there was never a place

where i wasn't yours:

parking lots

baseball fields

dance floors

bedrooms

daydreams.

i felt like yours

even when i wasn't.

is this how it feels?

when i look at you there are no butterflies,
only bees. or maybe the feeling of shaking
an etch a sketch after you were done
twisting all my buttons.

maybe this is what i've been looking for
when i wasn't paying attention.

in the snow

something about the summer makes me lonelier.
how there is more time on my hands left unheld.
maybe it's the dry heat that leaves me drained
even when the sun sets.
there's more room in the day to overthink.
it's about the nights that transition into the mornings
i wake up and realize no summer love is
destined for me this june and july.
when august comes i hang
my head on a rack as i search
for winter coats.
maybe the snow
will have something for me.

premature

i am afraid to make you laugh and hear
harmonies that lift me high enough to
run my fingers through the milky way
and tell all of jupiter's moons that i might
get to bring you up here with me.

silver lining

we have yet to break the edge of small talk
and i still can't figure out what color your eyes are,
too dark to determine. i catch myself leaning in and
i stop before i fall on the verge of your mouth,
one seat away and i don't know how to get closer.

we have yet to have a moment and i'm not sure
how it will sound.
i know how to make us cliché and how to tightrope
across the silver line.
i know how to make you pretty when i write

but i'm still figuring out how to make you mine.

the rush

my stomach is a butterfly garden that has
been closed since the last time there was
a reason for their wings to fly,

but i hear the glass start to crack when
our hands get too close for comfort.

i'll let this infatuation kill me if it means
i get to break the windows and set them all free.

i would even watch it shatter and shimmer if
it meant i got to spin you around as it fell apart.

the advent

yesterday i thought about you and it felt
like an honest mistake, human error.
i fold my hands like grandmother taught me and
recite a prayer insincerely; she forgives me.

today i thought about you and it felt like a betrayal,
like the eighth deadly sin. like all the churches closed
on sundays and i got cut on a stained-glass promise.
it only bleeds a little but never stops.

tomorrow i will probably think about you, and it will
feel like a new religion.
an archangel dressed in black and good intentions.
an almost-old testament of a love
that might be born again.

in dreams

i still like to write about people i know
i should not be writing about.
i know that i want to dream about the space above
and between us with the lights on,
but i don't want to have nightmares about
falling off the stratosphere.
i don't want to miss you the way i call my mother
after i've stopped breathing.
i want to die before everyone else i love.
i want to try and save the earth.
i want to smoke a cigarette for the placebo effect.
i don't want to think about my mother when i do it.
i want to believe in happy endings again.
i don't want to remember ruined castles.
i don't want to keep holding your spot in line
or checking the time and tapping my foot to the sound
of my heart cracking whenever i think you're on your way.

8:10 a.m.

i still shoot my shot into space and hope for the best.
i've fallen victim to sunburns and lightning that struck
too close to my feet, so i hope the sky is kinder when
i beg her to give me sun, especially in the mornings
when i look in your direction, a strip of green lights and
i'm not afraid to speed up i just

hope you never try to stop me.

onomatopoeia

small talk will crawl out of my mouth
on days when it looks like
you're about to say something

on days when you forget to take
one more look at me for the road

on days when you choose the seat next to me
only because you are closer to the door

i am tired of being a dandelion
and trying to get you to blow me away

our forte

i'll end up falling for you like snow,
slow and expected. you'll catch me
with your tongue and say my name
out loud for the first time and it will
sound like an orchestra with
more brass, more woodwinds,
more string and percussion.
it will feel like playing with fire,
knowing it will hurt but worth it
enough to find out how bad.

above

you look at me like i'm something
NASA is testing in the sky,
like i can be both beautiful and damned,
shiny and too far away to interpret.
like you would be willing to watch
me chase my dreams to jupiter
or crash down to earth when i don't
believe in myself enough to hold
my breath up there.
you look at me like you would
take me in any way that i came,

like you aren't afraid to catch a comet
with your bare hands.

wish for me

you are almost at the door

but turn around

to look once more;

i am a shooting star

that you cannot ignore.

when he said my hips were his favorite

you bore fruit when you leaned in / clementine lips
sprinkled citrus in all my wounds / it stung but the
burn made it feel all the more real / said my hips were
pumice / light in the right places and easy to spin around
/ surprised you liked my thin / that even my small
still filled your hands when you reached out / felt the
nervous and newly wrapped canvas but you liked me
in white / the virgin dressed in innocence with plenty of
introverted nights / and once the stage lights dimmed i
opened up like your bedside novel / my mouth was once
a library and you used to whisper when you entered /
then you tore down all the shelves and turned me into an
amphitheater and now you never fail to make me sing

fragile footing

you walk in the room

and all my guards fall down.

i'm a wind chime

and you're a tornado without warning

coming to spin me around.

lifetime of poetry

you gave me more in a september than
what i get on christmas day.
gave me enough hope to last me this far.
and i realize how you did just enough damage
so now i always have something to write about.

princess has arrived

i can't decide which one of us was in distress.
it's like we both needed some kind of saving.
i thought love was supposed to be wind in hair
and taste like summer did when we were children,
but each time i leave, it only makes the tower ache
for something to hold on to for one more forever.

you can't make a happy ending out of something
that only knows how to fall apart when it's over.

but if midnight keeps looking around and
the horses keep going wild trying to
figure out where all that longing is
coming from, just call out my name
and i'll be coming again.

this is where you stay

i like it when i meet
you in my dreams.
it's the only place now
where you don't leave.

in these dreams you are so ideal,
playing in a field that nobody knows of,
and i think we could have been real
if you had just simply shown up.

we softly grin from far away.
i bite at the nervous under my nails,
but this time i don't ask you to stay
and i don't miss you when you're gone.

you see, i love it when
i meet you in my dreams.
now i always get to be
the first to leave.

fooling myself

some days i promise that this isn't hopeless

sometimes i say i'm not breaking anymore

some days i wait for the door to open

sometimes i promise i'm not waiting

i knew i would see you again

there you are all handsome,
hair sticking up, never brushed,
and there i stand all in awe,
cotton mouth and blank thoughts,

words unable to string together
and hang up a sentence of confession,
how after these empty years
you're still invited to all my parties,

the ones with christmas lights
in obscure months and confetti
strewn all over the hardwood floors.
and we would tiptoe to your room,

lock the door with keys and hands
and finally touch after holding back,
swaddle you in arms that never
grew tired of holding your absence.

wanting in secret

you are all my daydreams and

i'm afraid that you will know,

so give me something to hold on to

when you're letting go.

before the band plays

when the crowd walks in, all face paint and confetti

with prideful alma maters and bent trombones,

i am still looking for you despite the noise.

i observe every face and tear the room apart

trying to find something that i always feel like i'm losing.

the room turns into an aquarium and everything is

floating and floating and when i find your laugh before

the drum line starts up again it is as though the world

is holding its breath, like it never wants to continue

spinning until you find my curious, desperate eyes.

some days i wonder if you are still looking,

and i can't tell if the world has started

rotating again without waiting for you

to find me.

right behind

a hundred wishbones
break at my hands
and hold every wish

we're by the door and
i almost taste your chapstick
but no goodbye kiss

and this time you
won't be someone
i learn how to miss

so if you go
then i am
coming with

baby, navy, and even midnight

i'll know i'm over you when

i stop wincing at blue.

when the sky and manhattan beach

don't swallow me in remembrance

of the only shade that feels like a breeze.

i'll know it has passed when i

stop looking for it in specks from afar.

i'll know it most especially

the day i forget what color

your eyes are.

high-school hopes

i danced through my seventeenth summer as i slowly
slipped into the autumn of his life / covered in earlier
sunsets and passionfruit tea / he left me in a winter that

lasted too long / watched him bloom in the remaining
seasons of what could have been our first spring and
every summer after that / though we never made it that
far /

had to grow new thorns and petals / learned how to
dance again / bare feet in the grass / cherishing this june /
drinking up her laugh / and all of her weekends

it still counts

they tell me not to touch this kind of love,

that it is dancing through rose thorns

and right below lightning storms,

but i'll meet it in car conversations

and pin-dropped locations

even if hearts

don't end up

collided.

i think it's still love

even if it's unrequited.

if it wasn't love
then why did it
feel like it was?

beautiful buds

go ahead and break my hands if it means
i'll stop planting what-ifs at your feet and
checking them every morning to see
if they grew at all overnight,

even the slightest bit.

the second time

i've never nose-dived out of the sky
but i know what it feels like when i fall asleep

i don't know what it's like to be called beautiful
but i know how to say it to myself and mean it

i haven't figured out how to stop myself from falling
but i'm glad to have tasted the courage to jump

the blues in your eyes aren't as light as his
but i know how to float in them still

i'm not sure if this is how love is supposed to look
but at least it feels like it

degas taught me

my heart is cracking beneath

your footsteps and i learned

ballet to the sound of its pieces

floating away.

in the distance

i'm told you will find it when you're least expecting,
when you're walking with your eyes closed
and arms crossed,
but how do i stop myself from looking?
my father reminds me of my age,
how i am just beginning my roaring twenties
and that there will be other cheeks to kiss
and more eyes to miss,
so why waste my time searching for something
i cannot predict?

i keep finding three-leaf clovers in my pockets,
i keep watching planes fly to see where
they're going to land,
i keep crossing the street and checking both ways.

things to be hopeful for

       (with confidence, with caution)

—for tomorrow, and tomorrow's tomorrow

—that my father's eyes will never dry out

—for my mother to feel twenty-one when she's fifty-one

—that i will get to where i have been trying to go

—for sea turtles to make it to the other side of the ocean

—that air won't run out and it will still taste good

—for the oceans to be free of plastic and human error

—that people will stop smoking cigarettes

—that people will start paying attention

—that you will come back

—that i will come back

what are you hopeful for?

(with confidence, with caution)

_____

_____

_____

_____

_____

_____

_____

_____

_____

_____

it will pass

it's been four years and
i'm still letting go,

so it might take a thousand
more tomorrows

before i move on
for the hundredth time,

but for now i'll let you
live free in my mind.

searching for signs

maybe you forgot when i told you everything.
when you asked for space on your birthday but
i gave you the world instead, and on the off days
i handed you the rest of the solar system and research
invested into finding something more infinite
than what i see when you look at me.
i dip my hands into black holes like empty pockets,
searching for loose change and sunflower seeds to
pull out as a peace offering or a shot in the dark.

maybe you will go and plant something i have
been trying to water for years now.
maybe something will bud if you
believe in it for once.

because you were the first

yes.

even now,

even when i shouldn't,

yes out loud and

in hallway whispers,

yes in the dark

and in public spaces,

yes in therapy

and blurry faces,

yes in every lifetime

where we could've worked,

yes on picked petals

and loose eyelashes.

yes,

even when it hurts.

a. yes

b. always

c. a and b

blonder days

my thoughts set up a blanket
in a park we swung in / i fall
again, like autumn leaves before
winter comes and takes it all
away from me / the day feels warm /
golden hour lasts longer than usual /
memories loop around the acre, and
laughter whistles in the wind that
took the candle's flame before you
made a wish / i say a bad joke and
all i remember are your dancing,
swirling eyes

forgetting

just because they
still live in your mind
tucked behind memories
and places they made room in
does not mean you haven't moved on.

it just means they stayed long enough
to carve initials under parts you can't see.
you are allowed to mourn their absence
without wishing for their return.

my turn

i misplace my grace

each time i see your lovely face

but these clouds turn gray

when i look your way

so perhaps it's time

to consider myself

and start chasing dreams

instead of someone else.

full control

that's it:
i'm putting the sun in every corner so that it
starts to hurt when i look up;

i'm pulling the tides up and over the x in the sand
so i stop believing i can find you easily;

i'm staring straight ahead while crossing the road so i
don't keep looking both ways for someone that isn't
coming;

i'm stomping on every dandelion so that i never
give another wish to summer's tongue.

i'll close my eyes when someone starts shooting
pretty stars so i can stop chasing things that fall
further away from me.

cautious

i am capsizing under you
but i am not sinking

this love is pulling me in
but i am not falling

i am doing this slowly and
with calculated movements

i am not this flickering spark
but i am the ballerina
i dreamed to become
the first time i even
thought about dancing
for someone other
than myself

therapy on 7th

who are all these sad songs i listen to for?
i used to curl into the holes of cellos
and warped wood violins,
but now i dance inside of flutes
and sounds of 80s synth.

the bar on 7th is telling me how to be alive
with catchy melodies and another sad song
by kelly clarkson, singing about how to breathe
for the first time since you've been gone.

who were all those i used to miss?
not one name comes to mind.

not even his.

buried

i believe i am still recovering.

i'm under the rubble and have stopped screaming.

been so used to having something

on top of me at all times

that my voice has forgotten how to ask for help.

how do you become something that

grows in between the cracks?

some days i can almost hear sirens in the distance.

i have to believe someone will save me eventually.

just getting started

learning to love this body

was like trying to push

through season one

before the show got good.

it was waiting for

the dough to rise,

for the sun to set,

for a new year's eve countdown.

it was being my own

best friend long enough

to understand how much

i deserve a love story too.

white dress

most nights

i am dressed

as the moon,

half empty

half full,

but some nights

i am all whole,

complete,

bright enough

to blind those

who thought

less of me,

big enough

to keep the sun

in hiding.

bigger

i used to tuck my knees in
on the plane ride home,
try not to take up as much space.
became an airplane bathroom,
all tight and cramped
and nowhere else to go.

but my knees felt the growing pains.

now i spread my legs when i sleep.
take up two seats on the bus.
make chairs push themselves in
as i walk through recklessly.
i don't need to fit anywhere.

i'll take up space in this
whole goddamn place.

self-care

being kind to myself

was a forgotten art.

learned to drag my

yesterdays by the wrist,

such a heavy reminder

not of where i once was

but where i am still going.

on track

i have to trust this universe

has some sort of plan for me,

that all these misguided moments

are supposed to put me on

the right track for the right things.

that this ferris wheel of hope

will one day bring me up to see

the view of something i never

even thought existed at all.

now i sleep in

on days you come in loud

like early morning construction,

i do my best to block out the sound

from the nights you stretched out

that ruined every one of my mornings,

but now i thankfully remember

how to live my life on days you're not around.

master of my alone

i've gone to bigger cities,

been swallowed by an even

bigger mouth.

i know how to hide in the dark,

but this lonely is not as cold as

people say it's supposed to be.

sometimes it's a blanket fort

or a bomb shelter.

it's safe and warm

and there are flowers in every corner

that do not die when i wake up.

turning twenty

the candle wax melts onto my cake as i look back
at the city i set on fire.
aspirations and checklists i set aside for tomorrow,
only to never complete them.

i blow out my candles and walk back to the ashes
with hopes to build a new resolution
where i do the things
i said i would do yesterday.

i'll repaint the city gold,
i'll turn on all the lights.

i've been to the sun once

to think about you still is a sin with no harm.
it feels like a blessing but doesn't make it right;
when you wave in the backdrop of my dreams
i whisper your name out of my own spite.

and if i had any self-control i would
return to every wild, infinite night,
but you already took me to the sun
and i don't need to go there twice.

my therapist told me to fly

the winter in me felt infinite,

but now i am the fox after hibernation,

the birds that return from the south,

the city of seattle under the sun.

warmth graces my skin like

it has been looking for me.

the tiny hairs across my limbs

stand tall, stretch out their bodies.

i think they feel it too.

what-if #1,118

there has to be a universe somewhere out there in which
we make it, where we end up in the way i always wrote
about, but not all good things happen how they are
supposed to.

there are hundreds of lifetimes where i could have
decided differently. where i could have just gone home
instead of taking you with me. or where i didn't ask you
to a dance or learn that song on piano. or where i didn't
keep saying yes despite having every reason not to.

even in all those multiverses where good things happen,
i know we still wouldn't have made it out hand in hand.

no amount of what-ifs can change back stars
from exploding and reigniting.
you can't make someone fall in love with you,
no matter how many times you dream
of doing yesterday differently.

to-do list for the lonely

— make a dinner reservation under your name, table for one

— order two glasses of wine then the whole damn bottle

— be the loudest person screaming during the scary movie

— clap when the plane lands for the cliché of being alive

— revisit the crosswalk where he went to the north pole

— run to the south pole so that you are the first to move on

— learn to swim in the deep end of the pool
        (let your head go under once)

— hum to the floorboards when the lonely gets too heavy

— laminate each promise and don't let them touch the floor

— remember every sad day is a monument to someplace much happier

how the scars healed

i hide behind books and the fear of being known again,

having to repeat my favorite things,

show you the wounds just to explain

why my hands look the way they do,

why i kiss with hesitation,

why i tell you to take it slow,

and why i close my eyes

when we pass by certain streets.

silence with ourselves

perhaps we learn
to love the lonely
even when we think
no one else will.

to sit in silence
on our long days,
to bathe in solidarity,
shut our eyes and smile
as we put our head under.

the luxury of solidarity

what a life to live,

to have not known love.

referred to as singular pronouns

but never as us.

at times i'm afraid to regret

the almosts

and the weight of

what could have been,

though i bask in

peace and relief

of a romance

that never happened.

still shining

i'm a disco ball spinning in a room
full of slow dancers and corsages,
first times and high heels lined up
against the wall, waiting to be claimed.
i sparkle in every light and rotate at my
own pace to whatever song is playing.
the slow dancers are blended together,
barely breathing, just leaning into
chests and shoulders but i am
still sparkling, still spinning,
even when the lights go out.

the brightest thing

when the dancing is across the room and you are still
a wallflower that only sways without being noticed /
know that you are greater than anyone who makes you
feel small / that you are a walking spotlight in an empty
auditorium

but there are people still cheering for you somewhere /
and others who have yet to see your grace someday will

/ i hope you never stop dancing on your own

out of the blue

don't plan for love that hasn't come;
they're on their way.

the quiet days and all the pain
are worth the wait.

they will come and you will fall
right into place.

and when love says they're here to stay,
they won't hesitate.

it's brave to be lost

we are asked who we want to be

when we grow up, and you can

hear every captive breath,

the humming hesitation,

the doubt.

you can still grow into

the person you wish to be

without waiting to grow up

or rushing too quickly.

it's okay if your futures

don't yet have a horizon,

to live life in pitch black.

those days will brighten.

wait and see

the sky will turn upside down
and alaska will break off from
her right-hand man before i ever stop
wondering if you're happy where you are.

your eyes close as the sun hides behind earth
and you probably never want to wake up.
your lungs are still looking for a way to breathe
for better reasons than just simply surviving.
your life is full of fruit and memories that have
spoiled, but have you thought about the ones
covered in sugar you have yet to live through?

pick your tomorrow

you don't have to wait
for new year's day
to start again

august has plenty of room
for you to be brand new

calendars will change
but you don't have to

you can grow at your own pace
no matter the date

look up

there could be
a storm on the way
that you cannot see
coming
nor know how
to run from

but you can still
look up and at least take
in the sky and her sun
while you still have it

love lights

i build myself a safe house that never hurts me,

but i keep staring out the window and looking out

at all the love lights in the distance,

all that wild freedom,

the rib-rubbed laughter,

the deliberate kisses

with hands that don't let go,

and if i were brave enough i would run to the lights, too,

ride the carousel and hold on for dear life.

sometimes i open the door to hear the music.

i may even step out on the porch

just to see the lights glisten.

by 2030

before the universe breaks apart

i'll find a face that looks

better moonlit than sun-kissed.

i'll be given the space it takes

for two people to fall safe,

and that face will keep the promises

you used to break.

the ones that never got enough daylight,

the ones you couldn't save.

i never even noticed

i think about how it doesn't hurt anymore.
how i only talk to you when it's your birthday.
how it seems that i've started to age like whiskey,
a slow, sweet burn.

i think about how much longer your hair got.
i think about you putting your hand on top
of mine while i reached for quarters to buy us coffee.

i think about how sweet i used to make my coffee.
i think about the way i asked if you felt the same,

the way you said no.

i think about the distance.
how long it took
to stop associating places with people.
to order coffee hot instead of iced,
to take it black and bitter.

i think about the notes and notions i left in a box.
i think about how i don't think of you.

sprouting

i stepped all over my gardens
to keep up with my mistakes,
to hold on to you without having to ask
and pleasing all those who never
earned the daisies i grew.

now there are thorns in
places that used to be softest
and holes in the ground where
i tried to bury myself breathing.

yesterday i found seeds in my pockets
and glove compartment
and behind my back teeth.
i will grow new gardens
once the sun comes back
and i tell her i won't leave
them to die this time.

convergence

the sky let down her hair and you climbed up to saturn.
walked in circles around her rings then placed one on
your finger.

when you were ready to go, you leaped, floated slowly
and gracefully. crashed down to earth, arriving so
dangerously and extraordinarily without fault or error
onto the asphalt i rode training wheels on. ran in circles
in search of the life that would fit in your gravity.

you'll find me in a parked car on top of an arizona
mountain and it won't feel like toronto or saturn's rings.
not even a san francisco breeze but perhaps
a new beginning.

if i am to find a love

so refreshing my father's

shoulders drop in relief,

the darling my mother

pictured me safe with,

the angel that all of

my friends root for,

the one that makes

me the kind of happy

i told my therapist

i wanted to be,

the love that i

keep writing about.

the uranometria at grand central station

i'm waiting the way i wait for spring and then summer,
for all of my tears to turn to mist

i'm waiting for a lifetime in which i do not write myself
into somebody else's world; they pen me first

i'm waiting for the 6 train in the middle of my life
to take me uptown or anywhere as long as i'm going up

i'm waiting for love like a carnation looking for sun,
but blooming is not an overnight miracle

i'm waiting for traffic lights to turn green
so that i can keep moving on

i don't know where i'm going
but at least i'm on my way

acknowledgments

an immense thank-you to all my friends and family
who have rooted for me throughout this entire process.
i would not have the confidence to release this without
your love.

thank you to those i've been honored to know in the
beautiful writing community. those who have given me
advice, feedback, a place to vent, a place to laugh. you
know who you are and the space you hold in my heart.

a lovely thank-you to Michelle Halket and Central
Avenue Publishing, for taking a chance on me and giving
this book a place to grow. you have given me a dream i
didn't think i could reach.

thank you to my readers who have stuck by me and
waited patiently for this collection. the support means
everything.

to the loves that inspired these works. thank you for not
falling for me. thank you for saying no. thank you for
saying yes. thank you for choosing someone else.

notes

"come look" was previously published in *The Tunnels*

"i knew i would see you again" was previously published in *The Tunnels*

"uncertainty" was previously published in *Milk + Beans*

"in the snow" was previously published in *Mohave He[art] Review*

"that laugh sounded like safety" was previously published in *Pulp Poets Press*

"and many more" was previously published in *Soft Cartel*

Zane Frederick grew up in the scorching valley that holds Phoenix, Arizona. After the release of his debut book, *(he)art.*, Zane matured in his writing to create his most recent and honest collection yet, *i am tired of being a dandelion*. A majority of this book was written during the summer he spent in New York City, in various coffee shops, street corners, and many hours at Grand Central Station.

Stay connected:

zanefrederickwrites.wixsite.com/poem

@zanefrederickwrites

zanefrederickwrites@gmail.com